LEVEL
3
Fact Reader

Amazon Animals

**100 FUN Facts
About Snakes,
Sloths, Spiders,
and More**

Rose Davidson

NATIONAL
GEOGRAPHIC

Washington, D.C.

For Emily, who braved the rainforest with me —R. D.

Published by National Geographic Partners, LLC, Washington, DC 20036.

Designed by Gus Tello

Photo Publisher's Note
The contents page features a red-headed poison frog (top), a toco toucan (bottom left), and a keel-billed toucan (bottom right).

The author and publisher gratefully acknowledge the expert content review of this book by Michael Malden, animal science manager of the "Amazon and Beyond" exhibits at Zoo Miami, as well as the literacy review of this book by Mariam Jean Dreher, professor emerita of reading education, University of Maryland, College Park.

Photo Credits
AL = Alamy Stock Photo; AS = Adobe Stock; GI = Getty Images; MP = Minden Pictures; NGIC = National Geographic Image Collection; NPL = Nature Picture Library; SS = Shutterstock
Cover, David A. Northcott/GI; header, FourLeafLover/AS; 1, nicostock/SS; 3 (UP RT), Dirk Ercken/SS; 3 (LO LE), Oleksiy Mark/SS; 3 (LO RT), Fedor Selivanov/SS; 4 (UP LE), Alex Hyde/NPL; 4 (UP RT), Avalon.red/AL; 4 (CTR LE), Pete Oxford/MP; 4 (CTR), pyty/AS; 4 (LO LE), benny-trapp/AS; 4 (LO RT), Pardofelis Photography/AL; 4-5, Gabrielle/AS; 5 (UP LE), guillaume regrain/GI; 5 (UP RT), Eric Isselée/AS; 5 (CTR), Doug Perrine/NPL; 5 (LO LE), Bence Mate/NPL; 5 (LO RT), wildarun/AS; 6-7, FG Trade/GI; 8 (LO), Robert Harding Picture Library/NGIC; 8 (UP), Rudzhan/AS; 9 (UP), Neil Ever Osborne/NGIC; 9 (LO), Jens/AS; 10 (UP), Nick Garbutt/NPL; 10 (LO), Felipe Cruz/GI; 11, rpbmedia/AS; 12, Martin Mecnarowski/AS; 13 (UP), Rebecca/AS; 13 (LO), Luke Massey/NPL; 14 (LO), barry b. doyle/GI; 14 (UP), AGAMI/AS; 15 (UP), swis-shippo/AS; 15 (CTR), Glenn Bartley/All Canada Photos/AL; 15 (LO), phototrip/AL; 16, Suzi Eszterhas/MP; 16-17, Lukas/AS; 18, David Tipling/Universal Images Group/Education Images/GI; 19, Bernard Castelein/NPL; 19 (LO), Milan/AS; 20 (LO), Edwin Butter/AS; 20 (UP), johan10/GI; 21 (UP), Eric Isselée/AS; 21 (LO), Thomas Marent/MP; 22, Piotr Naskrecki/MP; 23, Nick Hawkins/NPL; 24 (LO), Phil Savoie/NPL; 24 (UP), Chris Mattison/AL; 25 (UP LE), Nathan Shepard/GI; 25 (UP RT), Edwin Giesbers/NPL; 25 (LO), Arthur/AS; 26, Peter Schoen/GI; 27, Herve06/GI; 28-29, Sebastian Kennerknecht/MP; 28 (LO), Tiffany/AS; 29 (LO), Steve Winter/NGIC; 30 (UP), Edwin Giesbers/NPL; 30 (LO), Javier Fernández Sánchez/GI; 31 (UP), Ingo Arndt/MP; 31 (LO), Jason Edwards/NGIC; 32-33, Piotr Naskrecki/MP; 33, Mark Moffett/MP; 34 (UP), Robert Oelman/GI; 34 (LO), Peter Prokosch/Grid Arendal; 35 (UP), Morley Read/AL; 35, Nicky Bay; 36, ToniFlap/GI; 37 (UP), photocech/AS; 37 (LO), photocech/AS; 38 (UP), Carlos Grillo/AS; 38 (LO), tane-mahuta/GI; 39 (UP), Norbert Wu/MP; 39 (LO), Pulsar Imagens/AL; 40-41, Marcio Isensee e Sá/AS; 41 (UP RT), Rodrigo Costa Araújo/amazonmarmosets; 41 (LO RT), whitcomberd/AS; 42, Sue Cunningham/Worldwide Picture Library/AL; 43 (UP), Mike Mareen/AS; 43 (LO), Andres Pantoja/SOPA Images/GI; 44 (UP LE), Glenn Bartley/MP; 44 (UP), asbtkb/AS; 44 (CTR LE), The Natural History Museum/AL; 44 (CTR), Mark/AS; 44 (CTR RT), Bruce Thomson/NPL; 44 (LO RT), Jeff Cremer; 44 (LO), DS light photography/AS; 45 (UP RT), Redmond Durrell/AL; 45 (UP LE), Pete Oxford/MP; 45 (CTR), Pete Oxford/MP; 45 (CTR LE), Raphael Sane/Biosphoto/AL; 45 (CTR RT), Robert Oelman/GI; 45 (LO LE), phototrip.cz/AS; 45 (LO RT), Eric Isselée/AS

Library of Congress Cataloging-in-Publication Data
Names: Davidson, Rose, 1989- author.
Title: Amazon animals / Rose Davidson.
Description: Washington, D.C. : National Geographic Kids, [2023] | Series: National geographic readers | Includes index. | Audience: Ages 7-9 | Audience: Grades 2-3
Identifiers: LCCN 2022023689 (print) | LCCN 2022023690 (ebook) | ISBN 9781426372711 (paperback) | ISBN 9781426373329 (library binding) | ISBN 9781426374302 (ebook) |
Subjects: LCSH: Animals--Amazon River Region--Juvenile literature. | Rain forests--Amazon River Region--Juvenile literature. | Amazon River Region--Juvenile literature.
Classification: LCC QL237 .D38 2023 (print) | LCC QL237 (ebook) | DDC 591.98616--dc23/eng/20220706
LC record available at https://lccn.loc.gov/2022023689
LC ebook record available at https://lccn.loc.gov/2022023690

Printed in the United States of America
23/WOR/1

Contents

1
The one-inch-long bullet ant delivers the world's most painful insect sting.

2
Giant Amazon river turtles take turns cleaning each other's shells.

3
Kinkajous raid beehives in search of honey.

4
The sawlike edges on the toco toucan's bill allow it to peel fruit, such as oranges and figs.

5
The rufous potoo, a type of bird, hides by rocking its brown body back and forth to mimic a dead leaf blowing in the wind.

6
Glass frogs have see-through bodies.

7
The wings of a blue morpho butterfly can be about as wide as a soccer ball.

8
Pink-toed tarantulas defend themselves by kicking off sharp hairs that can be painful to predators.

9
Despite its name, the green iguana can also be orange, blue, or black.

10
The Amazonian giant centipede feeds on mice, lizards, frogs, and bats.

11
Green iguanas can survive a 40-foot fall.

12
The margay can run down trees headfirst.

25 COOL FACTS ABOUT AMAZON

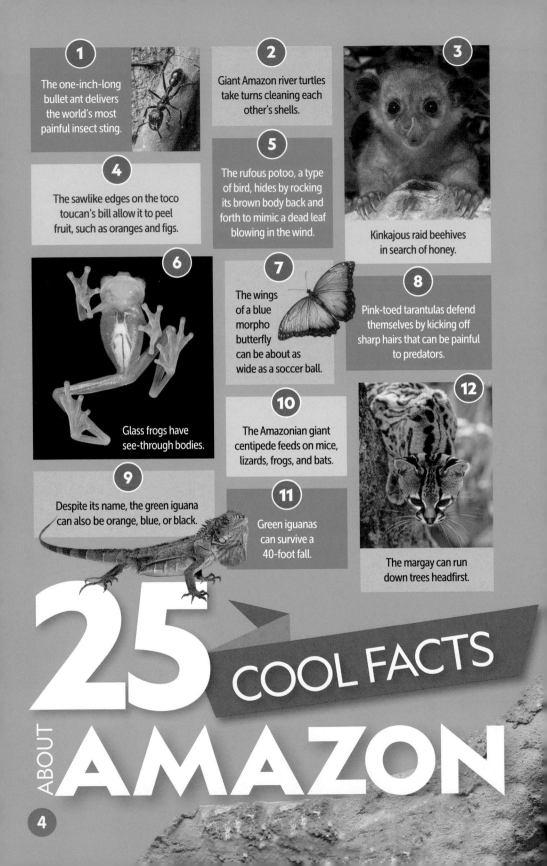

13 A giant anteater's spaghetti-shaped tongue is almost two feet long.

14 A bird called the hoatzin (wot-ZEEN) has claws on its wings when it's young.

15 The emperor tamarin was named after a German emperor who had a long, curly mustache.

16 Unlike other tapirs, the lowland tapir has a mohawk-like crest that runs along the back of its head.

17 The Amazonian manatee is the largest Amazon water animal and weighs more than 1,000 pounds.

18 The bald uakari (wuh-KAH-ree), a type of monkey, has a bright red face.

19 The green basilisk lizard can run across water.

20 The "howl" of the howler monkey sounds like a bark or a roar.

21 Giant armadillos can weigh more than 100 pounds. That's as much as a baby hippo!

22 Golden parakeets work together to raise groups of young.

23 Squirrel monkeys can leap sideways up to six feet.

24 Baby tapirs have stripes and spots to help them hide on the forest floor.

25 Amazon river dolphins can look pink.

ANIMALS

5

CHAPTER 1

The Amazing Amazon

The Amazon is home to MORE ANIMAL AND PLANT SPECIES than any other place on Earth.

Rain is falling. Drops of water roll off leaves and splat onto the forest floor. Birds call to one another from the treetops. In the distance, monkeys leap and the trees sway.

NORTH
AMERICA

AFRICA

SOUTH
AMERICA

Pacific
Ocean

Atlantic
Ocean

Southern Ocean
ANTARCTICA

NORTH
AMERICA

Amazon
River

SOUTH
AMERICA

PACIFIC
OCEAN

ATLANTIC
OCEAN

MAP KEY
Amazon
rainforest
Amazon
River

The Amazon rainforest stretches through eight countries in South America and one territory. The Amazon River runs through the middle of the forest. It is one of the world's largest and longest rivers.

About one of every 10 known species in the world LIVES IN THE AMAZON RAINFOREST.

On the ground, animals big and small find shelter from the rain. This is the Amazon rainforest. It is the biggest rainforest in the world.

Most rainforests have four layers. The tallest part, up at the treetops, is called the emergent layer. There, the wind is strong and the sun is bright. Birds soar through the trees or perch in the treetops to search for prey.

emergent layer

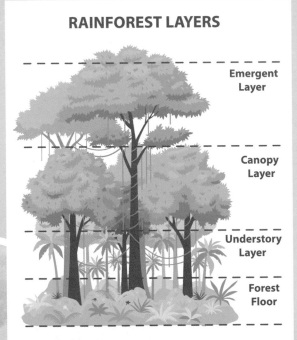

RAINFOREST LAYERS

Emergent Layer

Canopy Layer

Understory Layer

Forest Floor

Many rainforest animals move THROUGH THE LAYERS.

canopy layer

Below the emergent layer, the canopy layer is packed with branches and leaves. They give animals cover and shade. Monkeys and other tree-dwelling creatures hop from branch to branch, looking for food and a place to rest.

woolly monkey

9

The Amazon tree boa holds its body **IN AN S SHAPE** while waiting to **STRIKE AT PREY.**

understory layer

Beneath the canopy is the dense understory layer. It's filled with smaller trees and other plants. Here, jaguars and snakes blend in among the leaves. Frogs and salamanders like the warm, wet air, which keeps their skin from drying out.

South American river turtles **INSPIRED A LEGEND ABOUT A TURTLE-LIKE RIVER GODDESS.**

The lowest layer is the forest floor. Fallen leaves, bark, and twigs cover the ground. It bustles with activity, from small insects to giant rodents. In some parts of the forest, rivers flow across the floor. Animals swim or take a drink at the water's edge.

forest floor

Capybaras (kap-uh-BARE-uhz) can STAY UNDERWATER for up to FIVE MINUTES.

CHAPTER 2

In the Trees

Every macaw has a UNIQUE FACE PATTERN that makes it different from other macaws.

scarlet macaws

The Amazon's emergent and canopy layers are home to birds, sloths, monkeys, and many other animals. Macaws, a type of parrot, build their nests high in the trees.

These birds have colorful feathers and long tails. Their broad, pointed wings allow them to glide above the rainforest's tallest trees. They use their strong feet to grip branches when they rest and to hold on to tasty fruits and nuts.

blue-and-gold macaws

Macaws can fly up to 35 MILES AN HOUR— as fast as cars drive on neighborhood streets.

The hyacinth macaw's wingspan is LONGER THAN A GUITAR.

Birds live in all layers of the rainforest. But bigger birds live mostly in the top two layers.

LAUGHING FALCON: The laughing falcon lets out a *wah-ha-ha* sound when it's scared. Its favorite meal is snakes, which it hunts from the trees.

HARPY EAGLE: This bird of prey gets its name from a mythical monster with a bird's body and a woman's face. It eats sloths and monkeys in the canopy layer.

A harpy eagle's talons can be AS BIG AS A GRIZZLY BEAR'S CLAWS.

TOCO TOUCAN: The toco toucan is the biggest of all the different kinds of toucans in the toucan family. Its light, colorful bill helps it attract a mate.

SPECTACLED OWL: Active at night, the spectacled (SPEK-tuh-kuld) owl hunts for prey in the canopy layer. It has special feathers that funnel sound into its ears so it can pinpoint prey in the dark.

KING VULTURE: This scavenging bird soars high in the canopy layer, but it also visits the forest floor to dine on dead animals.

Like other vultures, king vultures can FLY FOR HOURS WITHOUT FLAPPING THEIR WINGS.

Most of the time, sloths rest in the trees of the canopy. They move so little, tiny green plants called algae (AL-jee) grow on their fur. Hanging among the leaves, the algae-covered animals are hard to spot. This helps them hide from hungry jaguars and birds.

When sloths do move in the trees, they are very slow. It can take a full minute for a sloth to move just a few feet! They're quicker in the water. They swim three times faster than they move on land.

Hoffmann's two-toed sloth

Sloths SLEEP FOR AROUND 10 TO 20 HOURS a day.

When they're thirsty, sloths drink DEW DROPS OFF LEAVES.

brown-throated three-toed sloth

17

Monkey Business

A howler monkey's call can be heard UP TO THREE MILES AWAY.

mantled howler monkey

Unlike slow and quiet sloths, howler monkeys are often on the move. They like to let other animals know they're around! They howl together as a troop, usually at dawn and dusk. Their loud calls sometimes tell other monkeys not to come too close. Other times, they howl to warn that a predator is nearby.

Bolivian red howler monkey

Howler monkeys are the loudest monkeys in the Amazon, and they're also the biggest. These standard poodle–size monkeys swing easily through the trees with long arms and hooklike hands.

A SPECIAL BODY PART in the howler monkey's throat makes its call LOUDER.

mantled howler monkey

Monkeys of many sizes live in the Amazon. Some are as long as a baseball bat, and others are as small as the palm of your hand.

CAPUCHIN MONKEY: Playful and smart, the capuchin (KAP-yuh-shin) is known for the "cap" of hair on its head. Female capuchins sometimes throw rocks at males to get their attention.

Capuchin monkeys sometimes USE ROCKS to crack open nuts.

GOLDEN LION TAMARIN: With a fiery orange mane, the golden lion tamarin looks like an African cat. Once there were just 200 of these monkeys in the wild. Now, thanks to protection efforts, there are more than 2,000!

PYGMY MARMOSET: The Amazon's smallest monkey is the pygmy marmoset. It stands about six inches tall, and it weighs less than an apple!

Marmosets usually give birth to TWINS.

SPIDER MONKEY: This primate has long, thin arms and a strong tail that can grasp branches. When it hangs upside down, it looks like a dangling spider.

CHAPTER 3

Under the Canopy

Vampire bats FEED ON THE BLOOD of other animals.

Unlike other types of bats, vampire bats CAN WALK, RUN, AND EVEN HOP ON ALL FOURS.

The understory and floor of the rainforest are humid and dark. Bats doze all day inside hollow trees in the understory. At night, they come out to eat.

In the Amazon, there are farms where people raise animals and grow plants. Vampire bats fly to these farms to feast on the blood of sleeping cows, pigs, and other animals. Heat sensors on the bats' noses guide them to warm blood vessels just below the animals' skin. Using their tiny, sharp teeth, the bats bite the animals without hurting them.

Poison frogs are tiny, colorful creatures. The flashy frogs can be yellow, gold, copper, red, green, blue, or black. Their bright colors and patterns warn other predators not to eat them.

blue poison frog

Scientists think poison frogs are TOXIC because of the BEETLES THEY EAT.

strawberry poison frog

In Colombia, the
native Emberá people
RUB THE TOXINS from
golden poison frogs
ON THEIR HUNTING
DARTS.

If predators
don't take the
hint, the frogs have a
nasty surprise. Poison in
their bodies makes the frogs taste
bad. These toxins can paralyze or
kill predators.

Most poison
frogs are the
SIZE OF A
PAPER CLIP.

25

Agoutis (uh-GOO-teez) are sometimes called JUNGLE GARDENERS.

On the forest floor, many animals play a part in keeping the forest healthy. Some animals eat decaying plants. Others drop food scraps that add nutrients to the soil.

Agoutis help new plants grow. These rabbit-size rodents collect nuts and seeds, and then bury them in the forest floor. If an agouti forgets about a buried stash, the seeds or nuts can sprout into plants. The new plants become part of the rainforest.

An agouti's coarse hair is covered in a STINKY, OILY LIQUID THAT REPELS WATER.

Agoutis can jump up to SIX FEET INTO THE AIR.

Kings of the Jungle

Jaguars are some of the biggest predators in the Amazon. And they are not picky eaters. They will eat almost anything, from tiny frogs to giant caimans (KAY-munz).

In the dark of night, jaguars listen and wait in the branches of the understory. When they spot their prey, they leap to the forest floor. Then, *chomp!* They use their strong jaws and sharp teeth to take down their prey.

In many ancient South American cultures, jaguars were WORSHIPPED AS GODS.

Unlike many other cats, jaguars are EXCELLENT SWIMMERS and will cross rivers to go after prey.

The jaguar is the LARGEST BIG CAT in the Western Hemisphere.

Jaguars have spots, called rosettes, that help them blend into their surroundings. For the rainforest's top predators, using camouflage (KAM-uh-flazh) helps them hide until their next meal comes along.

close-up of a jaguar's rosettes

The green anaconda is the **HEAVIEST SNAKE IN THE WORLD.**

Green anacondas sometimes **KILL AND EAT JAGUARS.**

The green anaconda is another sneaky predator. On land, it's easy to spot. But in the water, its patterned body blends in with plants. This helps it sneak up on fish, as well as mammals at the water's edge. The snake grabs its prey with its jaws. Then it wraps its body around the prey and squeezes until the prey is dead.

Creepy-Crawlies

Leafcutter ants carry pieces of plants almost **50 TIMES THEIR OWN WEIGHT.**

Leafcutter ants work as a team to carry pieces of leaves to their nest. But the leaves are not for eating. Instead, the ants use the leaves to "farm" their own food!

The
sawlike jaws of
leafcutter ants
VIBRATE A THOUSAND
TIMES A SECOND to
cut through
leaves.

Leafcutter ants
walk together in
lines that can reach
100 FEET LONG.

The ants build underground chambers and place a special fungus inside. Then they gather the leaves to feed the fungus. Once the fungus has grown, the ants feed it to their young.

Insects thrive on and near the rainforest floor. They come in all shapes and sizes.

ALLIGATOR BUG: The markings on this insect's head make it look like a reptile. The fake eyes and teeth might scare off predators.

More than 50,000 INSECT SPECIES can live inside a SINGLE SQUARE MILE of the Amazon.

GIANT JUMPING STICK: That's no stick—it's a grasshopper in disguise! The giant jumping stick has strong hind legs, so it can leap more than 10 times the length of its body.

ASSASSIN BUG: Like its name suggests, this species of insect lies in wait for prey before attacking. It uses a long, curved "beak" to stab its prey while holding it down with its legs.

Scientists think the Amazon could be home to about **2.5 MILLION INSECT SPECIES**—many still undiscovered.

JEWEL CATERPILLAR: This species might sparkle like jewels, but in fact, it's covered in spines of goo. The goo protects the caterpillar from hungry rainforest critters. If a predator grabs a spine, it breaks off so the caterpillar can escape.

Scary Swimmers

Up to 16 FEET LONG, the black caiman is THE BIGGEST OF ALL CAIMANS, which are closely related to alligators.

The rivers of the Amazon rainforest are filled with predators. The black caiman hunts at night. With only its eyes and nostrils above water, the reptile can sneak up on prey as it swims.

The giant river otter might be cute, but don't be fooled. This adorable animal is sometimes called the river wolf. Like wolves, these otters hunt in groups. A giant river otter can eat up to nine pounds of fish and other animals a day—about two to three times as much food as a human eats!

Giant river otters USE THEIR WHISKERS TO DETECT MOVEMENT in the water, similar to how cats detect movement on land.

What's lurking below the water's surface? Lots of fearsome fish swim in the Amazon's waters.

Some piranhas make BARK-LIKE SOUNDS to warn other fish to back off.

BULL SHARK: It's unusual to see sharks in a river, but bull sharks live in the rivers in the Amazon. Before attacking, the shark headbutts its prey, just like a bull. It eats fish, dolphins, and even other sharks.

RED-BELLIED PIRANHA: The red-bellied piranha (puh-RAH-nuh) is one of about 20 different species of piranha that swim in the Amazon. It has razor-sharp teeth. Most of its diet comes from the bitten-off fins of bigger fish.

ELECTRIC EEL: Special cells in the electric eel's body store power like tiny batteries. One species of eel can unleash 860 volts of power when it is scared or is attacking prey.

Arapaimas have a special body part that **ALLOWS THEM TO BREATHE AIR,** so they can survive outside of water for up to **24 HOURS.**

ARAPAIMA: One of the largest freshwater fish, the arapaima (air-uh-PIE-muh) commonly grows to be six feet long and weigh 200 pounds. But it is capable of reaching 15 feet and 440 pounds! It uses its mouth like a vacuum to suck in food, such as smaller fish.

CHAPTER 4

Saving the Rainforest

New animal and plant species are discovered in the Amazon EVERY OTHER DAY.

The Amazon is filled with wonders and many new things to discover. But human activities are hurting the Amazon. Fires burn down parts of the forest. Land is cleared for farming and cattle grazing, as well as for supplies of wood, oil, and metal. Animals are losing their homes, and special plants found only in the Amazon are disappearing.

Logs from rainforest trees are often used to make furniture and building materials.

But there's hope! People are working to save the rainforest and the animals that live there.

Scientists recently discovered a titi monkey that PURRS LIKE A CAT.

Schneider's marmoset

In 2021, a NEW SPECIES OF MARMOSET was found in a part of the forest that's quickly BEING CUT DOWN.

A machine clears rainforest land by taking down trees, which are then burned.

Laws now protect many parts of the Amazon from logging and other activities that destroy the forest. Satellites above the Amazon are tracking forest loss, so law officers can quickly step in to stop illegal activities. In addition, farmers are replanting trees. And people, just like you, are learning more about this incredible place and speaking up to ask leaders to protect it.

NEARLY HALF of the Amazon rainforest is PROTECTED.

This nursery in Brazil raises trees and other plants. They will be used for replanting the rainforest.

In this illustration, a satellite orbits Earth above the Amazon rainforest. Smoke from huge fires can be seen.

Together, we can help the Amazon rainforest and the amazing animals that call it home.

SAVE THE AMAZON

1 Macaws gather on cliffsides in Peru to lick clay for the salt that they need in their diet.

2 Female goliath bird-eating spiders sometimes eat their mates.

3 Emerald tree boas are born red or brown, and then turn green after a few months.

4 Scientists think fungus found on sloth hair could help cure cancer.

5 Surinam toads carry their eggs in pockets on their backs.

6 Tapirs use their fleshy trunks to grab leaves or act as snorkels in water.

7 Titan beetles can be almost as long as a toothbrush.

8 White-faced saki monkeys can leap more than 30 feet.

9 Glowworms on the rainforest floor can control when they light up, glowing brighter to lure prey.

10 Amazon milk frogs got their name for the white sticky substance they ooze through their skin.

11 Male red acouchis (uh-KOO-sheez), a type of rodent, make a high-pitched sound to attract females.

12 It takes a few days for a sloth to digest a single meal.

25 MORE FACTS ABOUT AMAZON

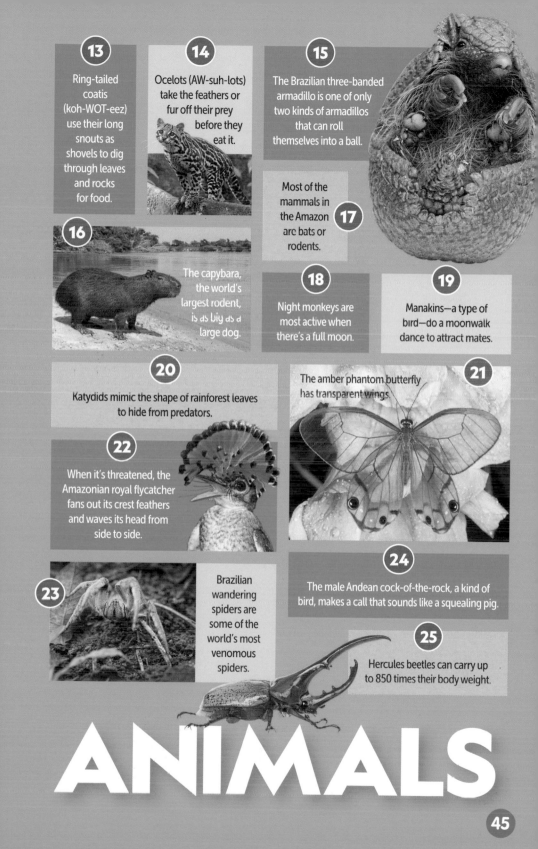

13

Ring-tailed coatis (koh-WOT-eez) use their long snouts as shovels to dig through leaves and rocks for food.

14

Ocelots (AW-suh-lots) take the feathers or fur off their prey before they eat it.

15

The Brazilian three-banded armadillo is one of only two kinds of armadillos that can roll themselves into a ball.

17

Most of the mammals in the Amazon are bats or rodents.

16

The capybara, the world's largest rodent, is as big as a large dog.

18

Night monkeys are most active when there's a full moon.

19

Manakins—a type of bird—do a moonwalk dance to attract mates.

20

Katydids mimic the shape of rainforest leaves to hide from predators.

21

The amber phantom butterfly has transparent wings.

22

When it's threatened, the Amazonian royal flycatcher fans out its crest feathers and waves its head from side to side.

24

The male Andean cock-of-the-rock, a kind of bird, makes a call that sounds like a squealing pig.

23

Brazilian wandering spiders are some of the world's most venomous spiders.

25

Hercules beetles can carry up to 850 times their body weight.

ANIMALS

Amazon Animals Facts Roundup

OOH, OOH, OOH! You've swung through all the Amazon animal info. Did you catch all 100 facts?

1. The one-inch-long bullet ant delivers the world's most painful insect sting. 2. Giant Amazon river turtles take turns cleaning each other's shells. 3. Kinkajous raid beehives in search of honey. 4. The sawlike edges on the toco toucan's bill allow it to peel fruit, such as oranges and figs. 5. The rufous potoo, a type of bird, hides by rocking its brown body back and forth to mimic a dead leaf blowing in the wind. 6. Glass frogs have see-through bodies. 7. The wings of a blue morpho butterfly can be about as wide as a soccer ball. 8. Pink-toed tarantulas defend themselves by kicking off sharp hairs that can be painful to predators. 9. Despite its name, the green iguana can also be orange, blue, or black. 10. The Amazonian giant centipede feeds on mice, lizards, frogs, and bats. 11. Green iguanas can survive a 40-foot fall. 12. The margay can run down trees headfirst. 13. A giant anteater's spaghetti-shaped tongue is almost two feet long. 14. A bird called the hoatzin has claws on its wings when it's young. 15. The emperor tamarin was named after a German emperor who had a long, curly mustache. 16. Unlike other tapirs, the lowland tapir has a mohawk-like crest that runs along the back of its head. 17. The Amazonian manatee is the largest Amazon water animal and weighs more than 1,000 pounds. 18. The bald uakari, a type of monkey, has a bright red face. 19. The green basilisk lizard can run across water. 20. The "howl" of the howler monkey sounds like a bark or a roar. 21. Giant armadillos can weigh more than 100 pounds. That's as much as a baby hippo! 22. Golden parakeets work together to raise groups of young. 23. Squirrel monkeys can leap sideways up to six feet. 24. Baby tapirs have stripes and spots to help them hide on the forest floor. 25. Amazon river dolphins can look pink. 26. The Amazon is home to more animal and plant species than any other place on Earth. 27. About one of every 10 known species in the world lives in the Amazon rainforest. 28. Many rainforest animals move through the layers. 29. Most rainforest animals live in the canopy. 30. The Amazon tree boa holds its body in an S shape while waiting to strike at prey. 31. South American river turtles inspired a legend about a turtle-like river goddess. 32. Capybaras can stay underwater for up to five minutes. 33. Every macaw has a unique face pattern that makes it different from other macaws. 34. Macaws can fly up to 35 miles an hour—as fast as cars drive on neighborhood streets. 35. The hyacinth macaw's wingspan is longer than a guitar. 36. A harpy eagle's talons can be as big as a grizzly bear's claws. 37. Like other vultures, king vultures can fly for hours without flapping their wings. 38. Sloths come down from the trees only about once a week to pee and poop. 39. Sloths sleep for around 10 to 20 hours a day. 40. When they're thirsty, sloths drink dew drops off leaves. 41. A howler monkey's call can be heard up to three miles away. 42. A special body part in the howler monkey's throat makes its call louder. 43. Capuchin monkeys sometimes use rocks to crack open nuts. 44. Marmosets usually give birth to twins. 45. Vampire bats feed on the blood of other animals.

46. Unlike other types of bats, vampire bats can walk, run, and even hop on all fours. 47. Vampire bats are so sneaky when they bite prey, sometimes the animals don't even wake up. 48. A vampire bat can recognize an animal's breathing pattern, so it can return to the same animal to feed again. 49. Poison frogs ooze toxic slime through their skin. 50. Scientists think poison frogs are toxic because of the beetles they eat. 51. In Colombia, the native Emberá people rub the toxins from golden poison frogs on their hunting darts. 52. Most poison frogs are the size of a paper clip. 53. Agoutis are sometimes called jungle gardeners. 54. Agoutis can jump up to six feet into the air. 55. An agouti's coarse hair is covered in a stinky, oily liquid that repels water. 56. Jaguars can kill their prey with a single bite. 57. In many ancient South American cultures, jaguars were worshipped as gods. 58. Unlike many other cats, jaguars are excellent swimmers and will cross rivers to go after prey. 59. The jaguar is the largest big cat in the Western Hemisphere. 60. The green anaconda is the heaviest snake in the world. 61. Green anacondas sometimes kill and eat jaguars. 62. Leafcutter ants carry pieces of plants almost 50 times their own weight. 63. The sawlike jaws of leafcutter ants vibrate a thousand times a second to cut through leaves. 64. Leafcutter ants walk together in lines that can reach 100 feet long. 65. More than 50,000 insect species can live inside a single square mile of the Amazon. 66. Scientists think the Amazon could be home to about 2.5 million insect species—many still undiscovered. 67. Up to 16 feet long, the black caiman is the biggest of all caimans, which are closely related to alligators. 68. Giant river otters use their whiskers to detect movement in the water, similar to how cats detect movement on land. 69. Bull sharks can live in both salt water and fresh water. 70. Some piranhas make bark-like sounds to warn other fish to back off. 71. Arapaimas have a special body part that allows them to breathe air, so they can survive outside of water for up to 24 hours. 72. New animal and plant species are discovered in the Amazon every other day. 73. Scientists recently discovered a titi monkey that purrs like a cat. 74. In 2021, a new species of marmoset was found in a part of the forest that's quickly being cut down. 75. Nearly half of the Amazon rainforest is protected. 76. Macaws gather on cliffsides in Peru to lick clay for the salt that they need in their diet. 77. Female goliath bird-eating spiders sometimes eat their mates. 78. Emerald tree boas are born red or brown, and then turn green after a few months. 79. Scientists think fungus found on sloth hair could help cure cancer. 80. Surinam toads carry their eggs in pockets on their backs. 81. Tapirs use their fleshy trunks to grab leaves or act as snorkels in water. 82. Titan beetles can be almost as long as a toothbrush. 83. White-faced saki monkeys can leap more than 30 feet. 84. Glowworms on the rainforest floor can control when they light up, glowing brighter to lure prey. 85. Amazon milk frogs got their name for the white sticky substance they ooze through their skin. 86. Male red acouchis, a type of rodent, make a high-pitched sound to attract females. 87. It takes a few days for a sloth to digest a single meal. 88. Ring-tailed coatis use their long snouts as shovels to dig through leaves and rocks for food. 89. Ocelots take the feathers or fur off their prey before they eat it. 90. The Brazilian three-banded armadillo is one of only two kinds of armadillos that can roll themselves into a ball. 91. The capybara, the world's largest rodent, is as big as a large dog. 92. Most of the mammals in the Amazon are bats or rodents. 93. Night monkeys are most active when there's a full moon. 94. Manakins—a type of bird—do a moonwalk dance to attract mates. 95. Katydids mimic the shape of rainforest leaves to hide from predators. 96. The amber phantom butterfly has transparent wings. 97. When it's threatened, the Amazonian royal flycatcher fans out its crest feathers and waves its head from side to side. 98. Brazilian wandering spiders are some of the world's most venomous spiders. 99. The male Andean cock-of-the-rock, a kind of bird, makes a call that sounds like a squealing pig. 100. Hercules beetles can carry up to 850 times their body weight.

INDEX